Series / Number 07-017

RELIABILITY AND VALIDITY ASSESSMENT

EDWARD G. CARMINES
Indiana University

RICHARD A. ZELLER
Bowling Green State University

SAGE PUBLICATIONS
The International Professional Publishers
Newbury Park   London   New Delhi

For information address:

SAGE Publications, Inc.
2455 Teller Road
Thousand Oaks, California 91320
E-mail: order@sagepub.com

SAGE Publications Ltd.
6 Bonhill Street
London EC2A 4PU
United Kingdom

SAGE Publications India Pvt. Ltd.
M-32 Market
Greater Kailash I
New Delhi 110 048 India

International Standard Book Number 978-0-8039-1371-4

Library of Congress Catalog Card No. L.C. 79-67629

10 11 12 13   35 34 33 32

When citing a university paper, please use the proper form. Remember to cite the Sage University Paper series title and include the paper number. One of the following formats can be adapted (depending on the style manual used):

(1) HENKEL, RAMON E. (1976) Tests of Significance. Sage University Paper Series on Quantitative Applications in the Social Sciences, 07-004. Newbury Park, CA: Sage.

OR

(2) Henkel, R. E. (1976). *Tests of significance* (Sage University Paper Series on Quantitative Applications in the Social Sciences, series no. 07-04). Newbury Park, CA: Sage.

CONTENTS

Editor's Introduction

RELIABILITY AND VALIDITY ASSESSMENT by Edward G. Carmines and Richard A. Zeller presents an elementary and exceptionally lucid introduction to issues in measurement theory. They define and discuss validity and reliability; proceed to a discussion of three basic types of validity, including criterion, content, and construct validity; present an introductory discussion of classical test theory, with an emphasis on parallel measures; and present a clear discussion of four methods of reliability estimation, including the test-retest, alternative-form, split-half, and internal consistency methods of reliability assessment. They conclude the text with a discussion of the use of reliability assessment for purposes of correcting bivariate correlations for attenuation due to random measurement error. All of this material is presented in such a way that the reader need only be familiar with simple correlational analysis in order to follow the presentation. The authors do a remarkable job of maintaining simplicity and lucidity of expression.

For the more advanced reader, Carmines and Zeller include an appendix which discusses the use of factor analysis in both reliability and validity assessment. To follow this discussion fully, the reader should have studied Kim and Mueller's earlier paper in this series, FACTOR ANALYSIS (number 14). This appendix discusses both theta and omega reliability estimation and then contrasts them with one another and with coefficient alpha, the most used method of internal consistency reliability estimation. Finally, the role of factor analysis in evaluating the validity of a set of measures is discussed, and the authors' final recommendation is that factor analysis be used in conjunction with the method of construct validation in order to establish the validity of any set of measures.

Although researchers in the fields of education and psychology have traditionally paid considerable attention to measurement theory, sociologists, political scientists, journalists, economists, and anthropologists have only recently begun to give these topics serious consideration. There is a burgeoning literature in these fields addressed primarily to overturning a number of previously accepted conclusions, based upon problems of validity and of reliability. Many of the conclusions in the political science literature of the previous two decades have, for example, recently been subjected to serious challenges on the grounds that the initial research was based on invalid and unreliable measurement procedures. And recent advances in statistical analysis, particularly those made in the use of maximum likelihood factor analysis, have drawn increasing attention to these nagging problems of measurement.

This introductory monograph is the perfect starting point for researchers in the above-named fields who wish to familiarize themselves with the current debates over appropriate measurement designs and strategies. In particular, researchers and students in the following fields will find this a convenient building block:

(1) social psychologists, who analyze personality, attitudes, and opinions

(2) psychologists and educators, who devise and administer achievement and ability tests

(3) sociologists, who study the attributes of individuals, as well as those who study aggregations, such as organizations and cultures

(4) political scientists, who study political behavior, political psychology, and public opinion (there is increased use of measurement theory among those who study international relations and comparative politics)

(5) journalists and mass media scholars, who study opinion polling and the impact of the mass media

(6) advertising specialists and public relations researchers, who examine cognitive structures and market preferences

(7) anthropologists, who study cultural differences and similarities between various aggregations, such as the nation-state, and who have a special interest in the cross-cultural validation of measurement procedures

(8) economists, who study consumer behavior and those who attempt to integrate measurement theory into their aggregate models of the economy.

All of these groups of scholars and practitioners should find the Carmines and Zeller monograph immensely useful in understanding the issues of measurement that increasingly dominate current debates in these fields. Although Carmines and Zeller do emphasize the use of reliability and validity assessment in the study of *individuals*, there is increasing attention to these issues among scholars who study various *aggregations*. This is particularly true when multiple measures of aggregate concepts are available for analysis, as in the literatures on American state politics, on cross-national variations in various demographic and political characteristics, and on administrative organizations in American life, to name just three obvious examples.

RELIABILITY AND VALIDITY ASSESSMENT is merely the first step toward understanding the complex issues of measurement in theoretical and applied research settings. The reader should supplement this with a careful reading of the two Kim and Mueller volumes in this series, INTRODUCTION TO FACTOR ANALYSIS and FACTOR ANALYSIS, and of course with the Sullivan and Feldman volume, MULTIPLE INDICATORS, which gives considerable attention to issues of validity and reliability. The Carmines and Zeller paper provides an excellent basis for understanding some of the more complex issues in measurement theory.

—John L. Sullivan, Series Editor

1. INTRODUCTION

Definition of Measurement

The notion that measurement is crucial to science seems a commonplace and unexceptional observation. Most book-length treatments of the philosophy of science include a discussion of the topic. And books focusing on research methods invariably have a chapter dealing with the problems associated with measurement. Yet, the widespread acknowledgment of the importance of good measurement has not—until quite recently—led to the development of systematic and general approaches to measurement in the social sciences. Quite the contrary, historically, measurement has been more of an abstract, almost ritualistic concern instead of being an integral and central aspect of the social sciences.

The coexistence of this asymmetric condition of ritualistic concern but lack of systematic attention with regard to measurement may be partially attributable to the way in which this term is most commonly defined. The most popular definition of measurement is that provided by Stevens more than 25 years ago. "Measurement," Stevens wrote, "is the assignment of numbers to objects or events according to rules" (1951: 22). The problem with this definition, from the point of view of the social scientist, is that, strictly speaking, many of the phenomena to be masured are neither objects nor events. Rather, the phenomena to be measured are typically too abstract to be adequately characterized as either objects or events.

Thus, for example, phenomena such as political efficacy, alienation, gross national product, and cognitive dissonance are too abstract to be considered "things that can be seen or touched" (the definition of an object) or merely as a "result, consequence, or outcome" (the definition of an event). In other words, Stevens's classical definition of measurement is much more appropriate for the physical than the social sciences. Indeed, it may have inadvertently impeded efforts to focus systematically on measurement in social research.[1]

A definition of measurement that is more relevant to the social sciences is that suggested by Blalock's observation that:

> Sociological theorists often use concepts that are formulated at rather high levels of abstraction. These are quite different from the variables that are the stock-in-trade of empirical sociologists. . . . The problem of bridging the gap between theory and research is then seen as one of measurement error [1968: 6; 12].

In other words, measurement is most usefully viewed as the "process of linking abstract concepts to empirical indicants" (Zeller and Carmines, forthcoming), as a process involving an "explicit, organized plan for classifying (and often quantifying) the particular sense data at hand—the indicants—in terms of the general concept in the researcher's mind" (Riley, 1963: 23).

This definition makes it clear that measurement is a process involving both theoretical as well as empirical considerations. From an empirical standpoint, the focus is on the *observable response*— whether it takes the form of a mark on a self-administered questionnaire, the behavior recorded in an observational study, or the answer given to an interviewer. Theoretically, interest lies in the *underlying unobservable* (and directly unmeasurable) *concept* that is represented by the response. Thus, using the above examples, the "mark" may represent one's level of self-esteem, the "behavior" may indicate one's level of personal integration during a conflict situation, and the "answer" may signify one's attitude toward President Carter. Measurement focuses on the crucial relationship between the empirically grounded indicator(s)—that is, the observable response—and the underlying unobservable concept(s). When this relationship is a strong one, analysis of empirical indicators can lead to useful inferences about the relationships among the underlying concepts. In this manner, social scientists can evaluate the empirical applicability of theoretical propositions. On the other hand, if the theoretical concepts have no empirical referents, then the empirical tenability of the theory must remain unknown. But what of those situations in which the relationship between concept and indicators is weak or faulty? In such instances, analysis of the indicators can lead possibly to incorrect inferences and misleading conclusions concerning the underlying concepts. Most assuredly, research based on such inadequate measurement models does not result in a greater understanding of the particular social science phenomenon under investigation. Viewed from this perspective, the *auxiliary theory* specifying the relationship between concepts and indicators is equally important to social research as the substantive theory linking concepts to one another.

Reliability and Validity Defined

Given the above definition of measurement, the question naturally arises as to how social scientists can determine the extent to which a particular empirical indicator (or a set of empirical indicators) represents a given theoretical concept. How, for example, can one evaluate the degree to which the four items used to measure political efficacy in *The American Voter* (Campbell et al., 1960) accurately represent that concept? Stated somewhat differently, what are the desirable qualities of any measuring procedure or instrument?

At the most general level, there are two basic properties of empirical measurements. First, one can examine the reliability of an indicator. Fundamentally, *reliability* concerns the extent to which an experiment, test, or any measuring procedure yields the same results on repeated trials. The measurement of any phenomenon always contains a certain amount of chance error. The goal of error-free measurement—while laudable—is never attained in any area of scientific investigation.[2] Instead, as Stanley has observed, "The amount of chance error may be large or small, but it is universally present to some extent. Two sets of measurements of the same features of the same individuals will never exactly duplicate each other" (1971: 356). Some particular sources of chance error will be discussed later in this chapter. For the moment it is simply necessary to realize that because repeated measurements never *exactly* equal one another, *unreliability* is always present to at least a limited extent. But while repeated measurements of the same phenomenon never precisely duplicate each other, they do tend to be consistent from measurement to measurement. The person with the highest blood pressure on a first reading, for example, will tend to be among those with the highest reading on a second examination given the next day. And the same will be true among the entire group of patients whose blood pressure is being recorded: Their readings will not be exactly the same from one measurement to another but they will tend to be consistent. This tendency toward consistency found in repeated measurements of the same phenomenon is referred to as *reliability*. The more consistent the results given by repeated measurements, the higher the reliability of the measuring procedure; conversely the less consistent the results, the lower the reliability.

But an indicator must be more than reliable if it is to provide an accurate representation of some abstract concept. It must also be valid. In a very general sense, any measuring device is valid if it does what it is intended to do. An indicator of some abstract concept is valid to the extent that it measures what it purports to measure. For example, the California F Scale (Adorno et al., 1950) is considered a valid measure of adherence to authoritarian beliefs to the degree that it does measure this theoretical concept rather than reflecting some other phenomenon. Thus, while reliability focuses on a particular property of empirical indicators—the extent to which they provide consistent results across repeated measurements—validity concerns the crucial relationship between concept and indicator. This is another way of saying that there are almost always theoretical claims being made when one assesses the validity of social science measures. Indeed, strictly speaking, one does not assess the validity of an indicator but rather the use to which it is being put. For example, an intelligence test may be valid for assessing the native intellectual potential of students, but it would not necessarily be valid for other purposes, such as forecasting their level of income during adulthood (Nunnally, 1978).

Just as reliability is a matter of degree, also is validity. Thus, the objective of attaining a perfectly valid indicator—one that represents the intended, and only the intended, concept—is unachievable. Instead, validity is a matter of degree, not an all-or-none property. Moreover, just because an indicator is quite reliable, this does not mean that it is also relatively valid. For example, let us assume that a particular yardstick does not equal 36 inches; instead, the yardstick is 40 inches long. Thus, every time this yardstick is used to determine the height of a person (or object), it systematically underestimates height by 4 inches for every 36 inches. A person who is six feet tall according to this yardstick, for example, is actually six feet eight inches in height. This particular yardstick, in short, provides an invalid indication of height. Note, however, that this error of 4 inches per yard will *not* affect the reliability of the yardstick since it does not lead to inconsistent results on repeated measurements. On the contrary, the results will be quite consistent although they will obviously be incorrect. In short, this particular yardstick will provide a quite reliable but totally invalid indication of height.

Random and Nonrandom Measurement Error

There are two basic kinds of errors that affect empirical measurements: random error and nonrandom error. Random error is the term used to designate all of those chance factors that confound the measurement of any phenomenon. The amount of random error is inversely related to the degree of reliability of the measuring instrument. To take a practical example, if a scale gives grossly inaccurate indications of the weight of objects—sometimes greatly overweighing them and other times underweighing them—then the particular scale is quite unreliable. Similarly, if the shots fired from a well-anchored rifle are scattered widely about the target, then the rifle is unreliable. But if the shots are concentrated around the target, then the rifle is reliable. Thus, a highly reliable indicator of a theoretical concept is one that leads to consistent results on repeated measurements because it does not fluctuate greatly due to random error.

While a formal discussion of random error and its affect on reliability estimation will be presented later in this volume, it is important for present purposes to make two observations about random error. First, indicators always contain random error to a greater or lesser degree. That is, the very process of measurement introduces random error to at least a limited extent. The distinction among indicators, therefore, is not whether they contain random error, but rather the extent to which they contain random error.

The second point that needs to be emphasized is that, as suggested above, the effects of random error are totally unsystematic in character. Referring to the earlier example of the rifle, random error would be indicated if the shots were as likely to hit above the target as below it or as likely to hit to the right of the target as to its left. Similarly, a scale that is affected by random error will sometimes overweigh a particular object and on other occasions underweigh it.

The specific sources of random measurement error that arise in the social sciences are too numerous to fully enumerate.[3] In survey research, the kinds of errors that may be assumed to be random include errors due to coding, ambiguous instructions, differential emphasis on different words during an interview, interviewer fatigue, and the like. But random error is not limited to survey research. It also arises in data collected from participant observations, content analysis, as well as simulations and experiments. Random measurement error is endemic to social research, as it is to all areas of scientific investigation including the physical and biological sciences.

The second type of error that affects empirical measurements is nonrandom error. Unlike random error, nonrandom error has a systematic biasing effect on measuring instruments. Thus, a scale that always registers the weight of an object two pounds below its actual weight is affected by nonrandom measurement error. Similarly, if a thermometer always registers 10 degrees higher than it should, then it is evidencing nonrandom measurement error. A third example of nonrandom measurement error can be given by slightly altering our earlier illustration focusing on the shots fired from a well-anchored rifle. If those shots aimed at the bull's eye hit approximately the same location but not the bull's eye, then some form of nonrandom error has affected the targeting of the rifle.

Nonrandom error lies at the very heart of validity. As Althauser and Heberlein observe, "matters of validity arise when other factors—more than one underlying construct or methods factors or other unmeasured variables—are seen to affect the measures in addition to one underlying concept and random error" (1970: 152; see also Werts and Linn, 1970). That is, invalidity arises because of the presence of nonrandom error, for such error prevents indicators from representing what they are intended to: the theoretical concept. Instead, the indicators represent something other than the intended theoretical concept—perhaps a different concept entirely. Thus, if a researcher uses a particular scale to represent ideological preference but later discovers that the scale actually taps party identification, then the scale is obviously an *invalid indicator of ideology*.

Just as reliability is inversely related to the amount of random error, so validity depends on the extent of nonrandom error present in the measurement process. For example, high scorers on the California F Scale (Adorno et al., 1950) have been shown to be persons who not only adhere to authoritarian beliefs but also "yea sayers" who agree with just about any assertion. In other words, the California F Scale seems to measure two different phenomena: adherence to authoritarian beliefs and the personality trait of acquiescence.[4] The California F Scale, in short, is not a totally valid measure of adherence to authoritarian beliefs. However, it would be a far less valid measure of this concept if later research concluded that the scale *only* measured acquiescence. This is another way of saying that validity, like reliability, is a matter of degree, and that it critically depends on the extent of nonrandom error in the measurement procedure (just as reliability depends on the amount of random error).

Conclusion

Reliability and especially validity are words that have a definite positive connotation. For anything to be characterized as reliable and valid is to be described in positive terms. So it is with any type of test, experiment, or measuring procedure. If it is reliable and valid, then it has gone a long way toward gaining scientific acceptance. Reliability concerns the degree to which results are consistent across repeated measurements. An intelligence test is quite reliable, for example, if an individual obtains approximately the same score on repeated examinations. Any measuring instrument is relatively reliable if it is minimally affected by chance disturbances (i.e., random measurement error). But empirical measures that are reliable have only come half way toward achieving scientific acceptance. They must also be valid for the purpose for which they are being used. Reliability is basically an empirical issue, focusing on the performance of empirical measures. Validity, in contrast, is *usually* more of a theoretically oriented issue because it inevitably raises the question, "valid for what purpose?" Thus, a driver's test may be quite valid as an indicator of how well someone can drive an automobile but it is probably quite invalid for many other purposes, such as one's potential for doing well in college. Validity, then, is evidenced by the degree that a particular indicator measures what it is supposed to measure rather than reflecting some other phenomenon (i.e., nonrandom measurement error).

In the beginning of this chapter we noted that, following Stevens, measurement is usually defined as the assignment of numbers to objects or events according to rules. But as we have seen, for any measuring procedure to be scientifically useful, it must lead to results that are relatively reliable and valid. In other words, viewed from a scientific perspective, it is crucial that the process of assigning numbers to objects or event leads to results that are generally consistent and fulfills its explicit purpose. The same point holds for Blalock's more social science oriented definition of measurement. Thus, for an indicator to be useful in social science research, it must lead to quite consistent results on repeated measurements and reflect its intended theoretical concept.

This chapter has outlined some basic considerations in measurement, especially in regard to the social sciences. The remaining chapters in this monograph will expand upon this discussion. Chapter 2 will consider the various types of validity thar are relevant in the social sciences. Chapter 3 will outline the logical, empirical, and statistical foundations of the theory of (random) measurement error, and Chapter 4 will discuss a variety of procedures for assessing the reliability of empirical measurements. Finally, the appendix will discuss and illustrate the role of factor analysis in assessing the reliability and validity of multiitem measures.

2. VALIDITY

In Chapter 1 we defined validity as the extent to which any measuring instrument measures what it is intended to measure. However, as we pointed out in Chapter 1, strictly speaking, "One validates, not a test, but an *interpretation of data arising from a specified procedure*" (Cronbach, 1971: 447). The distinction is central to validation because it is quite possible for a measuring instrument to be relatively valid for measuring one kind of phenomenon but entirely invalid for assessing other phenomena. Thus, one validates not the measuring instrument itself but the measuring instrument in relation to the purpose for which it is being used.

While the definition of validity seems simple and straightforward, there are several different types of validity that are relevant in the social sciences. Each of these types of validity takes a somewhat different approach in assessing the extent to which a measure measures what it purports to. The primary purpose of this chapter is to discuss the three most basic types of validity, pointing out their different meanings, uses, and limitations.

Criterion-Related Validity

Criterion-related validity (sometimes referred to as predictive validity) has the closest relationship to what is meant by the everyday usage of the term. That is, this type of validity has an intuitive meaning not shared by other types of validity. Nunnally has given a useful definition of criterion-related validity. Criterion-related validity, he notes, "is at issue when the purpose is to use an instrument to estimate some important form of behavior that is external to the measuring instrument itself, the latter being referred to as the criterion" (1978: 87). For example, one "validates" a written driver's test by showing that it accurately predicts how well some group of persons can operate an automobile. Similarly, one assesses the validity of college board exams by showing that they accurately predict how well high school seniors will do in college instruction.

The operational indicator of the degree of correspondence between the test and the criterion is usually estimated by the size of their correlation. Thus, in practice, for some well-defined group of subjects, one correlates performance on the test with performance on the criterion variable (this correlation, for obvious reasons, is sometimes referred to as a validity coefficient). Obviously the test will not be useful unless it correlates significantly with the criterion; and similarly, the higher the correlation, the more valid is this test for this particular criterion.[5]

We have said that the degree of criterion-related validity depends on the extent of the correspondence between the test and the criterion. It is important to realize that this is the *only* kind of evidence that is relevant to criterion-related validity. Thus, to take a rather unlikely example, "if it were found that accuracy in horseshoe pitching correlated highly with success in college, horseshoe pitching would be a valid measure for predicting success in college" (Nunnally, 1978: 88). The obtained correlation tells the entire story as regards criterion-related validity. Thus, criterion-related validity lends itself to being used in an atheoretical, empirically dominated manner. Nevertheless, theory usually enters the process indirectly because there must be some basis on which to select the criterion variables. Notice, further, that there is no single criterion-related validity coefficient. Instead, there are as many coefficients as there are criteria for a particular measure.

Technically, one can differentiate between two types of criterion-related validity. If the criterion exists in the present, then *concurrent validity* is assessed by correlating a measure and the criterion at the same point in time. For example, a verbal report of voting behavior could be correlated with participation in an election, as revealed by official voting records. *Predictive validity*, on the other hand, concerns a future criterion which is correlated with the relevant measure. Tests used for selection purposes in different occupations are, by nature, concerned with predictive validity. Thus, a test used to screen applicants for police work could be validated by correlating their test scores with future performance in fulfilling the duties and responsibilities associated with police work. Notice that the logic and procedures are the same for both concurrent and predictive validity; the only difference between them concerns the current or future existence of the criterion variable.

It is important to recognize that the scientific and practical utility of criterion validation depends as much on the measurement of the criterion as it does on the quality of the measuring instrument itself. This is sometimes overlooked in setting up and assessing validation procedures. Thus, in many different types of training programs, much effort and expense goes into the development of a test for predicting who will benefit from the program in terms of subsequent job performance. Take, for example, a managerial training program in which a screening test is used to select those few individuals who will be given supervisory responsibilities upon completion of the program. How is their subsequent performance—the criterion—measured? Often very little attention is given to the measurement of the criterion. Moreover, it is usually the case that subsequent performance is difficult to measure under the best of circumstances because, as Cronbach observes, "success on the job depends on nonverbal qualities that are hard to assess" (1971: 487). In short, those employing criterion validation procedures should provide independent evidence of the extent to which the measurement of the criterion is valid.[6] Indeed, Cronbach has suggested that "all validation reports carry the warning clause, 'Insofar as the criterion is truly representative of the outcome we wish to maximize'" (1971: 488).

As we have seen, the logic underlying criterion validity is quite simple and straightforward. It has been used mainly in psychology and education for analyzing the validity of certain types of tests and selection procedures. It should be used in any situation or area of scientific inquiry in which it makes sense to correlate scores obtained on a given test with performance on a particular criterion or set of relevant criteria.

At the same time, it is important to recognize that criterion validation procedures cannot be applied to all measurement situations in the social sciences. The most important limitation is that, for many if not most measures in the social sciences, there simply do not exist any relevant criterion variables. For example, what would be an appropriate criterion for a measure of a personality trait such as self-esteem? We know of no specific type of behavior that people with high or low self-esteem exhibit such that it could be used to validate a measure of this personality trait. Generalizing from this situation, it is not difficult to see that criterion validation procedures have rather limited usefulness in the social sciences for the simple reason that, in many situations, there are no criteria against which the measure can be reasonably evaluated. Moreover, it is clear that the more abstract the concept, the less likely one is to discover an appropriate criterion for assessing a measure of it. In sum, however desirable it may be to evaluate the criterion-related validity of social science measures, it is simply inapplicable to many of the abstract concepts used in the social sciences.

Content Validity

A second basic type of validity is content validity. This type of validity has played a major role in the development and assessment of various types of tests used in psychology and especially education but has not been employed widely by political scientists or sociologists. Fundamentally, content validity depends on the extent to which an empirical measurement reflects a specific domain of content. For example, a test in arithmetical operations would not be content valid if the test problems focused only on addition, thus neglecting subtraction, multiplication, and division. By the same token, a content-valid measure of Seeman's (1959) concept of alienation should include attitudinal items representing powerlessness, normlessness, meaninglessness, social isolation, and self estrangement. The above examples indicate that obtaining a content-valid measure of any phenomenon involves a number of interrelated steps. First, the researcher must be able to specify the full domain of content that is relevant to the particular measurement situation. In constructing a spelling test for fourth graders, for example, one must specify all of the words that a fourth grader should know how to spell. Second, one must sample specific words from this collection since it would be impractical to include all of these words in a single test. While it would be possible to select the sample of words for the test by simple random procedures, it might be important under certain circumstances to "oversample" particular types of words (e.g., nouns). Thus, the person constructing the test must be careful to specify the particular sampling procedures to be employed. Finally, once the words have been selected, they must be put in a form that is testable. For example, one might use a multiple-choice procedure whereby the correct spelling of the word would be included with several incorrect spellings with the students' having to choose the former. What should emerge from this process is a spelling test that adequately reflects the domain of content that is to be measured by the test.[7]

To take a different example, how would one go about establishing a content-valid measure of an attitude such as alienation? Presumably, one would begin by thoroughly exploring the available literature on alienation, hoping thereby to come to an understanding of the phenomenon. A thorough search and examination of the literature may suggest, for example, that alienation is properly conceived of in terms of the five dimensions proposed by Seeman: powerlessness, normlessness, meaninglessness, social isolation, and self estrangement. In addition, it may be useful to further subdivide these dimensions. One may want to subdivide powerlessness, for example, into its political, social, and economic aspects.

It is then necessary to construct items that reflect the meaning associated with each dimension and each subdimension of alienation. It is impossible to specify exactly how many items need to be developed for any particular domain of content. But one point can be stated with confidence: It is always preferable to construct too many items rather than too few; inadequate items can always be eliminated, but one is rarely in a position to add "good" items at a later stage in the research when the original pool of such items is inadequate.

From the above discussion, it should be clear that establishing a content-valid measure of an attitude such as alienation is far more difficult than establishing a content-valid achievement or proficiency test in some area (such as the spelling test above). There are two subtle but important differences between the two situations. First, however easy it may be to specify the domain of content relevant to a spelling test, the process is considerably more complex when dealing with the abstract concepts typically found in the social sciences. Indeed, it is difficult to think of any abstract theoretical concept—including alienation—for which there is an agreed upon domain of content relevant to the phenomenon. Theoretical concepts in the social sciences have simply *not* been described with the required exactness. The second, related problem is that, in measuring most concepts in the social sciences, it is impossible to sample content. Rather, one formulates a set of items that is intended to reflect the content of a given theoretical concept. Without a random sampling of content, however, it is impossible to insure the representativeness of the particular items.

These differences reveal quite clearly the rather fundamental limitations of content validity. In content validity, as Cronbach and Meehl observe, the "*acceptance* of the universe of content as defining the variable to be measured is essential" (1955: 282). As we have illustrated, however easy this may be to achieve with regard to reading or arithmetic tests, it has proved to be exceeding difficult with respect to measures of the more abstract phenomena that tend to characterize the social sciences. Second, there is no agreed upon criterion for determining the extent to which a measure has attained content validity. In the absence of well-defined, objective criteria, Nunnally has noted that "inevitably content validity rests mainly on appeals to reason regarding the adequacy with which important content has been sampled and on the adequacy with which the content has been cast in the form of test items" (1978: 93). Indeed, Bohrnstedt has argued that "while we enthusiastically endorse the procedures, we reject the concept of content validity on the grounds that there is no rigorous way to assess it" (forthcoming). In sum, while one should attempt to insure the content validity of any empirical measurement, these twin problems have prevented content validation from becoming fully sufficient for assessing the validity of social science measures.

Construct Validity

We have suggested that both criterion validity and content validity have limited usefulness for assessing the validity of empirical measures of theoretical concepts employed in the social sciences. It is partly for this reason that primary attention has been focused on construct validity. As Cronbach and Meehl observe, "Construct validity must be investigated whenever no criterion or universe of content is accepted as entirely adequate to define the quality to be measured" (1955: 282). Construct validity is woven into the theoretical fabric of the social sciences, and is thus central to the measurement of abstract theoretical concepts. Indeed, as we will see, construct validation must be conceived of within a theoretical context. Fundamentally, construct validity is concerned with the extent to which a particular measure relates to other measures consistent with theoretically derived hypotheses concerning the concepts (or constructs) that are being measured.

While the logic of construct validation may at first seem complicated, it is actually quite simple and straightforward, as the following example illustrates. Suppose a researcher wanted to evaluate the construct validity of a particular measure of self-esteem—say, Rosenberg's self-esteem scale. Theoretically, Rosenberg (1965) has argued that a student's level of self-esteem is positively related to participation in school activities. Thus, the theoretical prediction is that the higher the level of self-esteem, the more active the student will be in school-related activities. One then administers Rosenberg's self-esteem scale to a group of students and also determines the extent of their involvement in school activities. These two measures are then correlated, thus obtaining a numerical estimate of the relationship. If the correlation is positive and substantial, then *one piece of evidence* has been adduced to support the construct validity of Rosenberg's self-esteem scale.[8]

Construct validation involves three distinct steps. First, the theoretical relationship between the concepts themselves must be specified. Second, the empirical relationship between the measures of the concepts must be examined. Finally, the empirical evidence must be interpreted in terms of how it clarifies the construct validity of the particular measure.

It should be clear that the process of construct validation is, by necessity, theory-laden. Indeed, strictly speaking, it is impossible to "validate" a measure of a concept in this sense unless there exists a theoretical network that surrounds the concept. For without this network, it is impossible to generate theoretical predictions which, in turn, lead directly to empirical tests involving measures of the concept. This should not lead to the erroneous conclusion that only formal, fully developed theories are relevant to construct validation.

On the contrary, as Cronbach and Meehl observe:

> The logic of construct validation is involved whether the construct is highly systematized or loose, used in ramified theory or a few simple propositions, used in absolute propositions or probability statements [1955: 284].

What is required is that one be able to state several theoretically derived hypotheses involving the particular concept.

The more elaborate the theoretical framework, of course, the more rigorous and demanding the evaluation of the construct validity of the empirical measure. Notice that in the self-esteem example discussed above, we concluded that the positive association between Rosenberg's self-esteem scale and participation in school activities provided one piece of evidence supporting the construct validity of this measure. Greater confidence in the construct validity of this measure of self-esteem would be justified if subsequent analyses revealed numerous successful predictions involving diverse, theoretically related variables. Thus, construct validity is not established by confirming a single prediction on different occasions or confirming many predictions in a single study. Instead, construct validation ideally requires a pattern of consistent findings involving different researchers using different theoretical structures across a number of different studies.[9]

But what is a researcher to conclude if the evidence relevant to construct validity is negative? That is, if the theoretically derived predictions and the empirical relationships are inconsistent with each other, what is the appropriate inference? Four different interpretations are possible (Cronbach and Meehl, 1955). The most typical interpretation of such negative evidence is that the measure lacks construct validity. Within this interpretation, it is concluded that the indicator does not measure what it purports to measure. This does not mean, of course, that the indicator does not measure some other theoretical construct, but only that it does not measure the construct of interest. In other words, as negative evidence accumulates, the inference is usually drawn that the measure lacks construct validity as a measure of a particular theoretical concept. Consequently, it should not be used as an empirical manifestation of that concept in future research. Moreover, previous research employing *that* measure of the concept is also called into serious question.

Unfortunately, however, this is not the only conclusion that is consistent with negative evidence based on construct validation. Negative evidence may also support one or more of the following inferences.

First, the theoretical framework used to generate the empirical predictions is incorrect. To continue with the earlier example, it may be the case that, from a theoretical perspective, self-esteem should not be positively related to participation in school activities. Therefore, a nonpositive relationship between these variables would not undermine the construct validity of Rosenberg's self-esteem scale but rather cast doubt on the underlying theoretical perspective.

Second, the method or procedure used to test the theoretically derived hypotheses is faulty or inappropriate. Perhaps it is the case that, theoretically, self-esteem should be positively associated with participation in school activities and that the researcher has used a reliable and valid measure of self-esteem. However, even under these circumstances, the hypothesis will still not be confirmed unless it is tested properly. Thus, to take a simple example, the negative evidence could be due to the use of an inappropriate statistical technique or using the proper technique incorrectly.

Third, the final interpretation that can be made with respect to negative evidence is that it is due to the lack of construct validity or the unreliability of some other variable(s) in the analysis. In a very real sense, whenever one assesses the construct validity of the measure of interest, one is also evaluating simultaneously the construct validity of measures of the other theoretical concepts. In the self-esteem example, it could be the case that Rosenberg's self-esteem scale has perfect construct validity but that the measure of "participation in school activities" is quite invalid or unreliable.

Unfortunately, there is no foolproof procedure for determining which one (or more) of these interpretations of negative evidence is correct in any given instance. It is the total configuration of empirical evidence that lends credence to one interpretation rather than another. The first interpretation, that the measure lacks construct validity, becomes increasingly compelling as grounds for accepting the other interpretations become untenable. Most important, to the degree possible, one should assess the construct validity of a particular measure in situations in which the other variables are well-measured (i.e., have relatively high validity and reliability). Only in these situations can one confidently conclude that negative evidence is probably due to the absence of construct validity of a particular measure of a given theoretical concept.

Theoretically relevant and well-measured external variables are thus crucial to the assessment of the construct validity of empirical measurements (Curtis and Jackson, 1962; Sullivan, 1971, 1974; Balch, 1974). The logic of construct validation usually implies that the relationship among multiple indicators designed to represent a given theoretical concept and theoretically relevant external variables should be similar in terms of direction, strength, and consistency. For example, two indicators, both of which are designed to measure social status, should have similar correlations with political interest, if the latter is a theoretically appropriate external variable for the former. Conversely, if the two empirical indicators of social status relate differentially to external variables, this implies that the indicators are not representing the same theoretical concept. Instead, this pattern of empirical relationships would suggest that the two indicators represent different aspects of social status or different concepts entirely for they do not behave in accordance with theoretical expectations. It is thus easy to see that construct validation is enhanced if one has obtained multiple indicators of all of the relevant variables.[10]

Conclusion

In this chapter we have discussed the three basic types of validity: content validity, criterion-related validity, and construct validity. Both content validity and criterion-related validity have limited usefulness in assessing the quality of social science measures. Content validity, we argued, is not so much a specific type of validity as it is a goal to be achieved in order to obtain valid measurements of any type—namely, that the empirical measure covers the domain of content of the theoretical concept. Content validity, however, provides no method or procedure to determine the extent to which this goal is achieved in practice. Thus, in the final analysis, it is not possible to determine the specific extent to which an empirical measure should be considered content valid. On the contrary, content validity, by necessity, is an imprecise standard against which to evaluate the validity of empirical measurements.

Criterion-related validity is similarly limited regarding generalized applicability in the social sciences. This is *not* to argue that there are not certain practical circumstances under which it makes a good deal of sense to validate a measure by comparing performance on that measure with performance on a particular criterion variable. Thus, it is a reasonable strategy to compare airplane pilots' performance on a written examination with their ability to fly an airplane in order to validate the written exam. Yet, as we have pointed out, the vast majority of social science measures are *not* of this character. Instead, because they usually represent abstract theoretical concepts, there are no known criterion variables against which they can be compared.

In contrast to both content validity and criterion-related validity, construct validation has generalized applicability in the social sciences. The social scientist can assess the construct validity of an empirical measurement if the measure can be placed in theoretical context. Thus, construct validation focuses on the extent to which a measure performs in accordance with theoretical expectations. Specifically, if the performance of the measure is consistent with theoretically derived expectations, then it is concluded that the measure is construct valid. On the other hand, if it behaves inconsistently with theoretical expectations, then it is *usually* inferred that the empirical measure does not represent its intended theoretical concept. Instead, it is concluded that the measure lacks construct validity *for that particular concept*.

This chapter has focused on the different types of validity, pointing out their different meanings, uses, and limitations. The next chapter will present a theoretical framework that can be used to assess the reliability of empirical measurements.

3. CLASSICAL TEST THEORY

The purpose of this chapter is to present the foundations of a model for assessing random measurement error. This model is referred to as classical test score theory, classical test theory, or simply test theory. Our discussion of classical test theory is, by design, an elementary one. For much more extensive discussions of this general topic, see Lord and Novick (1968), Stanley (1971), and Nunnally (1978).

As we pointed out in Chapter 1, random error is involved in any type of measurement. Social scientists of course strive to eliminate as much random error from their measurements as possible, but even the most refined measuring instruments and techniques contain at least a limited amount of random error.

Reliability of Measurements

Since random error is an element that must be considered in the measurement of any phenomenon, we begin with the basic formulation

$$X = t + e \qquad [1]$$

where X is the observed score, t is the true score, and e is the random error. Equation 1 says simply that every observed score on any measuring instrument is made up of two quantities: a true score, one that would be obtained if there were no errors of measurement, and a certain amount of random error. While the meaning of an observed score is obvious, what is the nature of a true score and random error?

TRUE SCORES

Usually, true scores are conceived of as hypothetical, unobservable quantities that cannot be directly measured. Rather, a person's true score is the average score that would be obtained if the person were remeasured an infinite number of times on that variable.[11]

No single measurement would pinpoint the true score exactly but the average of an infinite number of repeated measurements would be equal to the true score. But since it is impossible to ever obtain an infinite number of repeated measurements but only a finite number, true scores are hypothetical, not real, qualities. Nevertheless, they are central to classical test theory and reliability estimation.

RANDOM ERROR

Equation 1 says that any particular observed score will not equal its true score because of random disturbances. These disturbances mean that on one testing occasion a person's obtained score would be higher than his true score while on another occasion his observed score would be lower than his true score. Moreover, the "positive" errors would be just as likely to occur as the "negative" errors, and their magnitudes would be similar as well. In short, the observed scores would be distributed symmetrically above and below the true score. Therefore, these errors are expected to cancel each other out in the long run—to have a mean or average score of zero. Intuitively, this is what is meant by random measurement error.[12]

These assumptions about true scores and random error can be represented more formally by the following equations: (a) the expected (mean) error score is zero: $E(e) = 0$; (b) the correlation between true and error scores is zero: $\rho_{(t,e)} = 0$; (c) the correlation between the error score on the measurement and the true score on a second is zero: $\rho_{(e_1,t_2)} = 0$; and (d) the correlation between errors on distinct measurements is zero: $\rho_{(e_1,e_2)} = 0$. In these assumptions, E represents the expected value or "long-run" mean of the variable and ρ is the correlation between two variables in a population. From these assumptions, most particularly assumption b above, it follows that the expected value of the observed score is equal to the expected value of the true score. In formula form: $E(X) = E(t) + E(e)$, but since $E(e) = 0$, then,

$$E(X) = E(t). \qquad\qquad [2]$$

The above results pertain to repeated measurements of a single variable for a single person. But reliability refers to the consistency of repeated measurements across persons rather than within a single person. Consequently, Equation 1 must be rewritten so that it does *not* pertain to a *single* observed score, true score, and random error but rather to the *variance* of those properties. Thus,

$$VAR(X) = VAR \, (t + e)$$

$$= VAR(t) + 2COV(t,e) + VAR(e).$$

But since assumption b above says that the correlation (and covariance) between true scores and errors is zero, then $2COV(t,e) = 0$. Consequently,

$$VAR(X) = VAR(t) + VAR(e). \qquad [3]$$

That is, the observed variance equals the sum of the true score and error variances. Given this, the ratio of true to observed variance

$$\rho_x = VAR(t)/VAR(X) \qquad [4]$$

is called the *reliability* of X as a measure of T. Reliability can also be expressed in terms of the error variance as follows:

$$\rho_x = 1 - [VAR(e)/VAR(X)] \qquad [5]$$

This equation follows directly from Equations 3 and 4 since

$$\rho_x = VAR(t)/VAR(X)$$

$$= [VAR(X) - VAR(e)]/VAR(X)$$

$$= 1 - [VAR(e)/VAR(X)].$$

Equation 5 makes it obvious that the reliability of a measure varies between 0 and 1. If all observed variance is contaminated with random error, then the reliability is zero since $1 - (1/1) = 0$. Conversely, if there is no random error involved in the measurement of some phenomenon, then the reliability equals 1 since $1 (0/1) = 1$. In sum, the greater the error variance, relative to the observed variance, the closer the reliability is to zero. But when the error variance approaches zero, then the reliability approaches unity. Finally, rearranging Equation 4, it is easy to see that

$$VAR(t) = VAR(X) \, \rho_x. \qquad [6]$$

That is, the true score variance of X equals the observed variance multiplied by the reliability of the measure. Thus, if one knew the reliability of a measure and its observed variance, then it would be easy to estimate its *unobserved* true score variance.

Parallel Measurements

The above discussion has pointed out what is meant by true scores and random error and has shown how reliability can be expressed in terms of the variances of these properties. But we have not yet described how one can estimate the reliability of a measure. This we propose to do in this section, showing that an estimate of a measure's reliability can be obtained by correlating parallel measurements.

Two measurements are defined as parallel if they have identical true scores and equal variances.[13] Symbolically, then, X and X' are parallel if $X = t + e$ and $X' = t + e'$ where $\sigma_e^2 = \sigma_{e'}^2$ and $t = t$. It may be useful to think of parallel measurements as being distinct from one another but similar and comparable in important respects. For example, consider the following two items from Rosenberg's (1965) self-esteem scale: (1) I feel that I have a number of good qualities and (2) I feel that I'm a person of worth, at least on an equal plane with others. A respondent with high self-esteem will usually answer "often true" while a respondent with low self-esteem will usually answer "seldom true" to these statements, except, of course, for random fluctuations. However, this is precisely the point. If the response to the items differ only with respect to random fluctuations, then the items are considered to be parallel. Parallel items are functions of the same true score and the differences between them are the result of purely random error.

The correlation between parallel measures can be expressed in terms of error, observed, and true scores as follows:

$$\rho_{xx'} = \sigma_{xx'}/\sigma_x\sigma_{x'} = \frac{\sigma_{(t+e)}\,\sigma_{(t+e')}}{\sigma_x\,\sigma_{x'}} = \frac{\sigma_t^2 + \sigma_{te} + \sigma_{te'} + \sigma_{ee'}}{\sigma_x\sigma_{x'}}. \quad [7]$$

Because, by assumption, errors are uncorrelated with true scores and uncorrelated with each other and the standard deviations of parallel measures are equal, this expression reduces to:

$$\rho_{xx'} = \sigma_t^2/\sigma_x^2. \quad [8]$$

The correlation between parallel measures is equal to the true score variance divided by the observed variance.

The imporance of this result is that it allows the unobservable true score variance to be expressed in terms of $\rho_{xx'}$ and σ_x^2—both of which are observable. In formula form:

$$\sigma_t^2 = \sigma_x^2\,\rho_{xx'}. \quad [9]$$

The true score variance is equal to the product of the observed variance and the correlation between parallel measures. Recalling from Equation 4 that reliability is $\rho_x = \sigma_t^2/\sigma_x^2$, it follows that the estimate of reliability is simply the correlation between parallel measures since

$$\rho_x = \sigma_t^2/\sigma_x^2 = \sigma_x^2\,\rho_{xx'}/\sigma_x^2 = \rho_{xx'}. \quad [10]$$

The result given in Equation 10 is quite important in estimating the reliability of empirical measurements. It indicates that if we have as few as two items of an single concept or a single item measured at two points in time, we can estimate the reliability of empirical measurements. It should also be clear that the greater the number of separate measurements of a given phenomenon, the more accurate (and higher) the estimate of its reliability will be. Of course this estimate will only be accurate if the items are actually parallel—that is, have identical true scores and equal error variances. It should also be noted that the correlation between the true and observed scores is equal to the square root of the reliability which, in turn, equals the square root of the correlation between parallel measures. That is,

$$\rho_{(t,x)} = \sqrt{\rho_x} = \sqrt{\rho_{xx'}} \,. \qquad [11]$$

Finally, it should be recognized that given the assumptions of classical test theory and the definition of parallel measures (for a proof see Lord and Novick, 1968) that

$$\rho_{xy} \leqslant \rho_{tx} = \sqrt{\rho_x} = \sqrt{\rho_{xx'}} \,, \qquad [12]$$

where y is any second measure and everything else is as above. That is, the correlation between a parallel measure and some other measure—for example, a particular criterion variable—cannot exceed the square root of the parallel measure's reliability. This means that the square root of the reliability of a measure provides an *upper bound* for its correlation with any other measure. For example, a measure with a reliability of .81 can never correlate greater than .9 with another variable. This demonstrates that reliability and *criterion-related* validity are closely related. Equation 12 also demonstrates that, as Bohrnstedt observes, "If one cannot reliably measure an attitude, he will never be able to predict actual behavior with it" (1970: 97).

Conclusion

This chapter has discussed the basic foundations of classical test theory, showing how it leads to the definition of reliability as being the ratio of the true to observed variance. The more true variance, relative to observed variance, the greater the reliability of the measure. We also showed that one way to estimate the reliability

of a measure is to compute the correlation between parallel measurements. In the next chapter we will discuss the different methods for
estimating the reliability of empirical measurements. These different methods are based on the logical foundations of classical
test theory, as outlined in this chapter.

4. ASSESSING RELIABILITY

In this chapter we discuss the four basic methods for estimating the reliability of empirical measurements. These are the retest method, the alternative-form method, the split-halves method, and the internal consistency method. This chapter also discusses how reliability estimates can be used to "correct" correlations for un-reliability due to random measurement error. Finally, we briefly evaluate the strengths and weaknesses of the various methods for assessing reliability.

Retest Method

One of the easiest ways to estimate the reliability of empirical measurements is by the retest method in which the same test is given to the same people after a period of time.[14] One then obtains the correlation between scores on the two administrations of the same test. The retest method is diagramed in Figure 1. It is presumed that responses to the test will correlate across time because they reflect the same true variable, t. The equations for the two tests may be written as follows:

$$X_1 = X_t + e_1 \qquad\qquad [13]$$

$$X_2 = X_t + e_2 \qquad\qquad [14]$$

But recalling that the definition of parallel measurements specifies that $t = t$ and $\sigma_{e_1}^2 = \sigma_{e_2}^2$ and that by the assumptions of classical test theory $\rho_{(e_1,t_2)} = 0$, and $\rho_{(e_1,e_2)} = 0$, it can be shown that

$$\rho_x = \rho_{x_1 x_2}, \qquad\qquad [15]$$

following exactly the same logic used to show that the correlation between parallel measures equals the reliability coefficient (see the derivation of Equation 10 above). That is, the reliability is equal to the correlation between the scores on the same test obtained at two points in time.

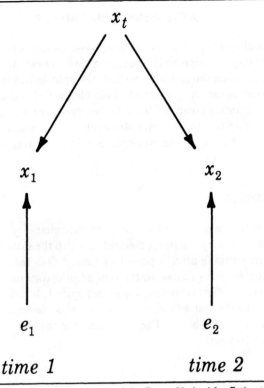

Figure 1: A Schematic Representation of the Retest Method for Estimating Reliability

If one obtains exactly the same results on the two administrations of the test, then the retest reliability coefficient will be 1.00. But, invariably, the correlation of measurements across time will be less than perfect. This occurs because of the instability of measures taken at multiple points in time. For example, a person may respond differently to a set of indicators used to measure self-esteem from one time to another because "the respondent may be temporarily distracted, misunderstand the meaning of an item," feel uncomfortable due to someone else being present, and so forth (Bohrnstedt, 1970: 85). All of these conditions reduce the reliability of empirical measurements.

While test-retest correlations represent an intuitively appealing procedure by which to assess reliability, they are not without serious problems and limitations. Perhaps most important, researchers are often only able to obtain a measure of a phenomenon at a single point in time. Not only can it be unduly expensive to obtain measurements at multiple points in time but it can be impractical as well. Even if test-retest correlations can be computed, their interpretation is not necessarily straightforward. A low test-retest correlation may not indicate that the reliability of the test is low but may, instead, signify that the underlying theoretical concept itself has changed. For example, one's attitude toward capital punishment may be very different before and after the person has viewed an execution. But true change is interpreted as measurement instability in the assessment of retest reliability. Moreover, the longer the time interval between measurements, the more likely that the concept has changed. In other words, a naive interpretation of test-retest correlations can drastically underestimate the degree of reliability in measurements over time by interpreting true change as measurement instability.[15]

A second problem that affects test-retest correlations and also leads to deflated reliability estimates is reactivity. Reactivity refers to the fact that sometimes the very process of measuring a phenomenon can induce change in the phenomenon itself. Thus, in measuring a person's attitude at time 1, the person can be sensitized to the subject under investigation and demonstrate a change at time 2, which is due solely to the earlier measurement. For example, if a person is interviewed about the likelihood of voting in an approaching election at time 1, the person might decide to vote (at time 2) and cast a ballot (at time 3) merely because he or she has been sensitized to the election. In this case, the test-retest correlation will be lower than it would be otherwise because of reactivity.

While the test-retest correlations can certainly underestimate the reliability of empirical measurements, the more typical problem is overestimation due to memory. For example, the person's memory of his responses during the first interview situation is quite likely to influence the responses which he gives in the second interview. In other words, if the time interval between measurements is relatively short, the subjects will remember their earliest responses and will appear more consistent than they actually are. Memory effects lead to inflated reliability estimates. In fact, Nunally believes that "during the two-week's to one-month's time in which it is advisable to complete both testings, memory is likely to be a strong factor, thus, the retest method will often provide a substantial overestimate of what would be obtained from the alternative-form method" (1964: 85).

Alternative-Form Method

The alternative-form method is used extensively in education to estimate the reliability of all types of tests. In some ways, it is similar to the retest method in that it also requires two testing situations with the same people. However, it differs from the retest method in one very important regard: The same test is not given on the second testing but an alternative form of the same test is administered. These two forms of the test are intended to measure the same thing. Thus, for example, the two tests might focus on arithmetical operations with each containing 25 problems that are at approximately the same level of difficulty. Indeed, the two forms should *not* differ from each other in any systematic way. One way to help insure this is to use random procedures to select items for the different forms of the test. The correlation between the alternative forms provides the estimate of reliability. It is recommended that the two forms be administered about two weeks apart, thus allowing for day-to-day fluctuations in the person to occur (Nunnally, 1964).

The alternative-form method for assessing reliability is obviously superior to the simple retest method, primarily because it reduces the extent to which individuals' memory can inflate the reliability estimate. However, like the retest method, the alternative-form method when used for only two testing administrations does not allow one to distinguish true change from unreliability of the measure. For this reason, the results of alternative-form reliability studies are easier to interpret if the phenomenon being measured is relatively enduring, as opposed to being subject to rapid and radical alteration.

The basic limitation of the alternative-form method of assessing reliability is the practical difficulty of constructing alternative forms that are parallel. It is often difficult to construct one form of a test much less two forms that display the properties of parallel measurements.

Split-Halves Method

Both the retest and the alternative-form methods for assessing reliability require two test administrations with the same group of people. In contrast, the split-halves method can be conducted on one occasion. Specifically, the total set of items is divided into halves and the scores on the halves are correlated to obtain an estimate of reliability. The halves can be considered approximations to alternative forms.

As a practical example, let us assume that a teacher has administered a six-word spelling test to his students and would like to determine the reliability of the total test. He should divide the test into halves, determine the number of words that each student has spelled correctly in each half, and obtain the correlation between these scores. But as we have determined previously, this correlation would be the reliability for each half of the test rather than the total test. Therefore, a statistical correction must be made so that the teacher can obtain an estimate of the reliability of the six-word test, not just the three-word half tests. This "statistical correction" is known as the Spearman-Brown prophecy formula, derived independently by Spearman (1910) and Brown (1910). In particular, since the total test is twice as long as each half, the appropriate Spearman-Brown prophecy formula is:

$$\rho_{xx''} = \frac{2\rho_{xx'}}{1 + \rho_{xx'}}$$

where $\rho_{xx''}$ is the reliability coefficient for the whole test and $\rho_{xx'}$ is the split-half correlation. Thus, if the correlation between the halves is .75, the reliability for the total test is:

$$\rho_{xx''} = [(2) (.75)]/(1 + .75) = 1.50/1.75 = .857.$$

The estimated reliability of the six-item test is .857. It is not difficult to see that the split-half reliability varies between 0 and 1, taking on these limits if the correlation between the halves is .00 or 1.00, respectively.

The more general version of the Spearman-Brown prophecy formula (of which Equation 16 is a special case) is:

$$\rho_{x_n x_n''} = N\rho_{xx'} / [1 + (N-1)\rho_{xx'}]. \qquad [17]$$

This gives the reliability of a scale which is N times longer than the original scale. Thus, if the reliability of the original scale is .40, then a scale five times that long has a reliability of .77 as follows:

$$\rho_{n_n x_n''} = 5(.40) / [1 + (5-1).40]$$

$$= 2 / 2.6$$

$$= .77.$$

To take another example, if a five-item split-half correlates .2 with another five-item split-half, then the estimated reliability for a scale four times that long would equal .5 as follows:

$$\rho_{x_n x_n''} = 4(.2) / [1 + (4-1)(.2)]$$

$$= .8 / 1.6$$

$$= .5.$$

"This means that, if one form of a test composed of 5 items correlates .2 with a parallel form of that test that also has 5 items, then a form composed of 20 items similar to the initial 5 should correlate .5 with a parallel form containing 20 items" (Stanley, 1971: 395).

By rearranging Equation 17 one can also determine the number of items that would be needed to attain a given reliability or what the split-half must be, given a desired reliability and test length. To estimate the number of items required to obtain a particular reliability, one uses the following formula:

$$N = \rho_{xx''}(1 - \rho_{xx'}) / \rho_{xx'}(1 - \rho_{xx''}),$$ [18]

where $\rho_{xx''}$ is the desired reliability; $\rho_{xx'}$ is the reliability of the existing test; and N is the number of times test would be lengthened to obtain reliability of $\rho_{xx''}$. Thus, if a 10-item test has a reliability of .60, then the estimated lengthening required to obtain a reliability of .80 would be:

$$N = .8(1 - .6) / .6(1 - .8)$$

$$= 2.7.$$

In other words, approximately 27 items would be required to reach a reliability of .80.

There is a certain indeterminancy in using the split-halves technique to estimate reliability due to the different ways that the items can be grouped into halves. The most typical way to divide the items is to place the even-numbered items in one group and the odd-numbered items in the other group. But other ways of partitioning the total item set are also used including separately scoring the first and second halves of the items and randomly dividing the items into two groups. In fact, for a 10-item scale, there are 125 different possible splits. The point is that each split will probably result in a slightly different correlation between the two halves which, in turn, will lead to a different reliability estimate. Moreover, since the number of different splits is a function of the number of total items, obtaining a consistent estimate of reliability increases as the number of items increases. Thus, using the split-halves method, it is quite probable that different reliability estimates will be obtained—even though the same items are administered to the same individuals at the same time.

Internal Consistency Method

We noted above that an important limitation of the split-halves method of assessing reliability is that reliability coefficients obtained from different ways of subdividing the total set of items would not be the same. For example, it is quite possible that the correlation between the first and second halves of the test would be different from the correlation between odd and even items. However, there are methods for estimating reliability that do not require either the splitting or repeating of items. Instead, these techniques require only a single test administration and provide a unique estimate of reliability for the given test administration. As a group, these coefficients are referred to as measures of internal consistency. By far the most popular of these reliability estimates is given by Cronbach's alpha (Cronbach, 1951), which can be expressed as follows:

$$\alpha = N/(N - 1) [1 - \Sigma\sigma^2(Y_i)/\sigma_\chi^2] \qquad [19]$$

where N is equal to the number of items; $\Sigma\sigma^2(Y_i)$ is equal to the sum of item variances; and σ_χ^2 is equal to the variance of the total composite. If one is working with the correlation matrix rather than the variance-covariance matrix, then alpha reduces to the following expression:

$$\alpha = N\bar{\rho}/[1 + \bar{\rho}(N - 1)] \qquad [20]$$

where N is again equal to the number of items and $\bar{\rho}$ is equal to the mean interitem correlation. To take a hypothetical example applying Equation 20, if the average intercorrelation of a six-item scale is .5, then the alpha for the scale would be:

$$\alpha = 6(.5)/[1 + .5(6 - 1)]$$

$$= 3 / 3.5$$

$$= .857.$$

To give an example of how alpha is calculated, consider the 10-item self-esteem scale developed by Rosenberg (1965). The intercorrelations among the items for a sample of adolescents are presented in Table 3 (for further discussion of these data see the appendix). To find the mean interitem correlation we first sum the

45 correlations in Table 3: .185 + .451 + .048 + . . . + .233 = 14.487. Then we divide this sum by 45: 14.487/45 = .32. Now we use this mean interitem correlation of .32 to calculate alpha as follows:

$$\alpha = 10(.32)/[1 + .32(10 - 1)]$$

$$= 3.20 \ / \ 3.88$$

$$= .802.$$

From Equation 20 it is not difficult to see that alpha varies between .00 and 1.00, taking on these limits when the average interitem correlations are zero and unity, respectively.

The interpretation of Cronbach's alpha is closely related to that given for reliability estimates based on the split-halves method. Specifically, coefficient alpha for a test having 2N items is equal to the average value of the alpha coefficients obtained for all possible combinations of items into two half-tests (Novick and Lewis, 1967). Alternatively, alpha can be considered a unique estimate of the expected correlation of one test with an alternative form containing the same number of items. Nunnally (1978) has demonstrated that coefficient alpha can also be derived as the expected correlation between an actual test and a *hypothetical* alternative form of the same length, one that may never be constructed.

Novick and Lewis (1967) have proven that, in general, alpha is a *lower bound* to the reliability of an unweighted scale of N items, that is, $\rho_x \geqslant \alpha$. It is equal to the reliability if the items are parallel. Thus, the reliability of a scale can never be lower than alpha even if the items depart substantially from being parallel measurements. In other words, in most situations, alpha provides a conservative estimate of a measure's reliability.

Equation 20 also makes clear that the value of alpha depends on the average interitem correlation and the number of items in the scale. Specifically, as the average correlation among items increases and as the number of items increases, the value of alpha increases. This can be seen by examining Table 1 which shows the value of alpha given a range in the number of items from 2 to 10 and a range in the average interitem correlation from .0 to 1.0. For example,

TABLE 1

Values of Cronbach's Alpha for Various Combinations of Different
Number of Items and Different Average Interitem Correlations

Number of Items	Average Interitem Correlation					
	.0	.2	.4	.6	.8	1.0
2	.000	.333	.572	.750	.889	1.000
4	.000	.500	.727	.857	.941	1.000
6	.000	.600	.800	.900	.960	1.000
8	.000	.666	.842	.924	.970	1.000
10	.000	.714	.870	.938	.976	1.000

a 2-item scale with an average iteritem correlation of .2 has an alpha of .333. However, a 10-item scale with the same average interitem correlation has an alpha of .714. Similarly, an 8-item scale with an average interitem correlation of .2 has an alpha of .666 whereas if the 8 items had an average intercorrelation of .8, then the scale's alpha would be .970. In sum, the addition of more items to a scale that do *not* result in a reduction in the average interitem correlation will increase the reliability of one's measuring instrument.

While increasing the number of items in a scale can thus improve the scale's reliability, there are significant limitations to this procedure. First, the adding of items indefinitely makes progressively less impact on the reliability. Thus, given an average interitem correlation of .4, increasing the number of items from 2 to 4 increases the alpha for the scale by .155 (i.e., .727 − .572 = .155). However, increasing the number of items from 8 to 10 with the same average interitem correlation only increases the alpha by .028 (i.e., .870 − .842 = .028). Second, the greater the number of items in a scale, the more time and resources are spent constructing the instrument. It should be noted, finally, that adding items to a scale can, in some instances, *reduce* the lengthened scale's reliability if the additional items substantially lower the average interitem correlation.

Alpha is more difficult to compute than coefficients based on other methods of assessing reliability. In the retest, alternative-form, and split-halves methods, it is only necessary to calculate a single correlation to obtain the desired reliability estimate. Specifically, in the retest method, scores for the same group of people on the same test administered on two occasions are correlated; in the alternative-forms approach, scores on different versions of the same test are correlated; and in the split-halves method, the items are divided into arbitrary halves and scores between the half-tests are correlated. In contrast, as we have seen, alpha depends on the average inter-correlation among all of the items. Yet, it is important to realize that although more complex computationally, alpha has the same logical status as coefficients arising from the other methods of assessing reliability. This is easy to see once we consider some additional properties of parallel measurements. In addition to having equal true scores and equal error variances, parallel measurements are assumed to have the following useful properties:

(1) The expected (mean) values of parallel measures are equal: $E(X) = E(X')$.
(2) The observed score variance of parallel measures is equal: $\sigma_x^2 = \sigma_{x'}^2$.
(3) The intercorrelations among parallel measurements are equal from pair to pair: $\rho_{xx'} = \rho_{xx''} = \rho_{x'x''}$.
(4) The correlations of parallel measures with other variables are equal: $\rho_{xy} = \rho_{x'y} = \rho_{x''y}$.

These properties imply that there are no systematic differences between parallel measurements; instead, they only differ from another because of strictly random error, and thus, for essential purposes, are completely interchangeable. Moreover, since parallel measurements have equal intercorrelations, the average interitem correlation is simply equal to the correlation between any arbitrary pair of items. In other words, *if the items are truly parallel*, the average inter-item correlation accurately estimates all of the correlations in the item matrix. Thus, *logically*, using the average correlation in the calculation of alpha amounts to exactly the same thing as calculating a simple correlation between parallel measurements.

KR20

Cronbach's alpha is a generalization of a coefficient introduced by Kuder and Richardson (1937) to estimate the reliability of scales composed of dichotomously—scored items. Dichotomous items are scored one or zero depending on whether the respondent does or does not possess the particular characteristic under investigation. Thus, for the items making up a spelling test, a score of 1 would be given when the students spelled a particular word correctly but zero if the word is spelled incorrectly. To determine the reliability of scales composed of dichotomously scored items, one uses the following Kuder-Richardson formula number 20 (symbolized KR20):

$$KR20 = N/(N-1) \, [1 - \Sigma p_i q_i / \sigma_x^2] \qquad [21]$$

where N is the number of dichotomous items; p_i is the proportion responding "positively" to the ith item; q_i is equal to $1 - p_i$; and σ_x^2 is equal to the variance of the total composite. Since KR20 is simply a special case of alpha, it has the same interpretation as alpha; that is, it is an estimate of the expected correlation between one test and a hypothetical alternative form containing the same number of items.

Correction for Attenuation

Whatever particular method is used to obtain an estimate of reliability, one of its important uses is to "correct" correlations for unreliability due to random measurement error. That is, if we can estimate the reliability of each variable, then we can use these estimates to determine what the correlation between the two variables would be if they were made perfectly reliable. The appropriate formula is as follows:

$$\rho_{x_t y_t} = \rho_{x_i y_j} / \sqrt{\rho_{xx'} \rho_{yy'}} \qquad [22]$$

where $\rho_{x_t y_t}$ is the correlation corrected for attenuation; $\rho_{x_i y_j}$ is the observed correlation; $\rho_{xx'}$ is the reliability of X; and $\rho_{yy'}$ is the reliability of Y. For example, if the observed correlation between two variables was .2 and the reliability of each variable was .5, then the correlation corrected for attentuation would be:

$$\rho_{x_t y_t} = .2/\sqrt{(.5)(.5)} = .4.$$

This means that the correlation between these two variables would be .4 if both were perfectly reliable (measured without random error).

Table 2 illustrates the behavior of the correlation coefficient under varying conditions of correction for attenuation. Table 2A shows the value of the correlation corrected for attenuation given that the observed correlation is .3 with varying reliabilities of X and Y. As an example, when the reliabilities of X and Y are .4, respectively, the corrected correlation is .75. When the reliabilities of X and Y are 1.0, respectively, the corrected correlation is equal to the observed correlation of .3. Table 2B presents similar calculations when the observed correlation is .5. Examining sections A and B of Table 2 it is clear that the higher the reliabilities of the variables, the less the corrected correlation differs from the observed correlation.

Table 2C presents the value of the correlation that one will observe when the correlation between X_t and Y_t is .5 under varying conditions of reliability. If the reliabilities of X and Y are .8, respectively, the observed value of a theoretical .5 correlation is .4. Table 2D presents similar calculations when the correlation between X_t and Y_t is .7. For example, even if the theoretical correlation between X_t and Y_t is .7, the observed correlation will be only .14 if the reliabilities are quite low (.2). Thus, one must be careful not to conclude that the theoretical correlations are low simply because their observed counterparts are low; it may instead be the case that the measures are quite unreliable.

Conclusion

This chapter has discussed four methods for assessing the reliability of empirical measurements. For reasons mentioned in the chapter, neither the retest method nor the split-halves approach is

TABLE 2
Examples of Correction for Attenuation

A: $\rho_{x_t y_t} = .3/\sqrt{\rho_{xx'}\rho_{yy'}}$

			$\rho_{xx'}$		
	.2	.4	.6	.8	1.0
.2	—	—	.87	.75	.67
.4	—	.75	.61	.53	.47
$\rho_{yy'}$ .6	.87	.61	.50	.43	.39
.8	.75	.53	.43	.38	.33
1.0	.67	.47	.39	.33	.30

B: $\rho_{x_t y_t} = .5/\sqrt{\rho_{xx'}\rho_{yy'}}$

			$\rho_{xx'}$		
	.2	.4	.6	.8	1.0
.2	—	—	—	—	—
.4	—	—	—	.88	.79
.6	—	—	.83	.72	.65
.8	—	.88	.72	.63	.56
1.0	—	.79	.65	.56	.50

C: $.5 = \rho_{xy}/\sqrt{\rho_{xx'}\rho_{yy'}}$

			$\rho_{xx'}$		
	.2	.4	.6	.8	1.0
.2	.10	.14	.17	.20	.22
.4	.14	.20	.24	.28	.32
$\rho_{yy'}$ .6	.17	.24	.30	.35	.39
.8	.20	.28	.35	.40	.45
1.0	.22	.32	.39	.45	.50

D: $.7 = \rho_{xy}/\sqrt{\rho_{xx'}\rho_{yy'}}$

			$\rho_{xx'}$		
	.2	.4	.6	.8	1.0
.2	.14	.20	.24	.28	.31
.4	.20	.28	.34	.40	.44
$\rho_{yy'}$ .6	.24	.34	.42	.48	.54
.8	.28	.40	.48	.56	.63
1.0	.31	.44	.54	.63	.70

recommended for estimating reliability. The major defect of the retest method is that experience in the first testing usually will influence responses in the second testing. The major problem with the split-halves approach is that the correlation between the halves will differ somewhat depending on how the total number of items is divided into halves. As Nunnally argues, "it is best to think of the corrected correlation between any two halves of a test as being an *estimate* of coefficient alpha. Then it is much more sensible to employ coefficient alpha than any split-half method" (1978: 233).

In contrast, the alternative-form method and coefficient alpha provide excellent techniques for assessing reliability. The practical limitation of using the alternative-form method is that it can be quite difficult to construct alternative forms of a test that are parallel. One recommended way of overcoming this limitation is by randomly dividing a large collection of items in half to form two randomly parallel tests. In sum, if it is possible to have two test administrations, then the correlation between alternative forms of the same test provides a very useful way to assess reliability.

Coefficient alpha should be computed for any multiple-item scale. It is particularly easy to use because it requires only a single test administration. Moreover, it is a very general reliability coefficient, encompassing both the Spearman-Brown prophecy formula as well as the Kuder-Richardson 20. Finally, as we have seen, alpha is easy to compute, especially if one is working with a correlation matrix (for further details on the computation of alpha see Bohrnstedt, 1969). The minimal effort that is required to compute alpha is more than repaid by the substantial information that it conveys about the reliability of a scale. What is a satisfactory level of reliability? Unfortunately, it is difficult to specify a single level that should apply in all situations. As a general rule, we believe that reliabilities should not be below .80 for widely used scales. At that level, correlations are attenuated very little by random measurement error. At the same time, it is often too costly in terms of time and money to try to obtain a higher reliability coefficient. But the most important thing to remember is to report the reliability of the scale and how it was calculated. Then other researchers can determine for themselves whether it is adequate for any particular purpose.

NOTES

1. Stevens's definition of measurement is considerably less stringent than some earlier definitions, which proposed that the term be restricted to the assignment of numbers to objects or events only when there exist operations upon the objects or events similar to the arithmetic operations upon the numbers. For a brief but lucid discussion of various efforts to define measurement, see Jones (1971).

2. It may seem that it is possible (even quite likely) that repeated measurements of some attributes, especially physical attributes, would exactly duplicate each other. But as Stanley has aptly stated, "the discrepancies between two sets of measurements may be expressed in miles and, in other cases, in millionths of a millimeter; but, if the unit of measurement is fine enough in relation to the accuracy of the measurements, discrepancies always will appear" (1971: 356).

3. For a comprehensive listing of various factors that contribute to error variance and systematic variance in educational testing, see Stanley (1971).

4. For discussions of the conflicting evidence concerning acquiescence, see Bentler et al. (1972) and Rorer (1967).

5. Nunnally (1978) argues that even modest correlations (e.g., a correlation of .30) between test and criterion can prove quite useful for selection purposes. He also argues that the "proper way to interpret a validity coefficient is in terms of the extent to which it indicates a *possible improvement in the average quality of persons* that would be obtained by employing the instrument in question" (1978: 91).

6. As we will discuss later in this volume, random measurement error always attenuates simple correlations. In other words, low validity coefficients can result from substantial unreliability in either the measuring instrument or the critierion variable. Therefore, a low validity coefficient does not necessarily mean that the measuring instrument and/or the criterion are invalid; instead, it may indicate that substantial random error affects either or both measurements. It is especially useful to obtain independent evidence concerning the extent of the reliability of the criterion variable, although its measurement is often neglected in practical situations.

7. Sometimes the term "face validity" is used in the social sciences. This type of validity should not be confused with content validity. Face validity, as Nunnally (1978: 111) has noted, "concerns judgements about an instrument *after* it is constructed," focusing on the extent to which it "looks like" it measures what it is intended to measure. Thus, face validity is, at best, concerned with only one aspect of content validity.

8. It is important to realize that the size of this correlation will depend on the reliability and validity of *both* measures. Thus, in assessing construct validity, it is important to obtain independent evidence concerning the reliability and validity of the "second" measure. The situation is the same as that involved in evaluating criterion-related validity, as discussed above (see Note 6).

9. There are very few published studies in which construct validation is the central concern of the analysis. For a useful example see Hofstetter's (1971) careful analysis of the construct validity of the "amateur politician."

10. Campbell and Fiske's (1959) concepts of convergent and discriminant validity can be seen as a logical extension of construct validity in which each of the constructs is measured by *multiple methods*. Convergent validity refers to the extent to which different methods of measuring the same trait yield similar results; the fundamental assumptions being that different methods of measuring the same trait should converge on the same result. Discriminant validity, on the other hand, refers to the extent to which similar or identical methods measuring different traits lead to different results; that is, discriminant validity implies that traits that are truly distinct from one another should lead to different results even if they are measured by the same method. For a discussion of how convergent and discriminant validity are analyzed within the multitrait-multimethod matrix, see Sullivan and Feldman (1979).

11. In formal terms, this "average score" is referred to as the expected value (or mean) if someone were remeasured an infinite number of times on that variable.

12. In formal terms, random error can be defined as error that has a definite (usually equal) probability of occurring in the long run.

13. Parallel measurements have a number of other interesting properties but these are not central for the development here. For further discussion, see Lord and Novick (1968). It is worth noting that many of the results presented here apply not only to parallel measurements but also to tests or items that are tau-equivalent, essentially tau-equivalent, or congeneric. Measurements are tau-equivalent if they have identical true scores but possibly different error variances. Measurements are essentially tau-equivalent if their true scores differ by an additive constant. And measurements are congeneric if their true scores are linearly dependent on each other. Thus, the most restrictive measurement model is the parallel model whereas the least restrictive is the congeneric model. For further discussion of these models, see Greene and Carmines (forthcoming), Jöreskog (1971), Lord and Novick (1968), and Novick and Lewis (1967).

14. A variety of other terms (e.g., items, indicators) could be used in place of tests here with no loss of generality to the discussion.

15. While it is impossible to separate true change from unreliability in the retest method, Heise (1969) has shown that this can be obtained if there are at least three occasions on which the variable is measured and if one is willing to make certain simplifying assumptions. For further discussion of methods for assessing the reliability and stability of measurements over time, see Achen (1975), Wheaton et al. (1977), Wiley and Wiley (1970), Wiley and Wiley (1974), and Erikson (1978).

16. Our discussion of the role of factor analysis in reliability and validity assessment only provides an introduction to this rather complex topic. For more thorough discussions see Carmines and Zeller (1974), Zeller and Carmines (1976, forthcoming), Greene and Carmines (forthcoming), Allen (1974), Armor (1974), Heise and Bohrnstedt (1970), Smith (1974a, 1974b), Jöreskog (1971), and Bentler (1969).

17. For a thorough discussion of the methods of factor analysis, see Harman (1976). Kim and Mueller's (1978a, 1978b) volumes on factor analysis in this series provide a very useful introduction to the topic.

REFERENCES

ACHEN, C. W. (1975) "Mass political attitudes and the survey response." American Political Science Review 69: 1218-1231.

ADORNO, T. W., E. FRENKEL-BRUNSWIK, D. J. LENISON, and R. N. SANFORD (1950) The Authoritarian Personality. New York: Harper & Row.

ALLEN, M. P. (1974) "Construction of composite measures by the canonical-factor regression method," pp. 51-78 in H. L. Costner (ed.) Sociological Methodology 1973-1974. San Francisco: Jossey-Bass.

ALTHAUSER, R. P. and T. A. HERBERLEIN (1970) "Validity and the multitrait-multimethod matrix," pp. 151-169 in E. F. Borgatta and G. W. Bohrnstedt (eds.) Sociological Methodology 1970. San Francisco: Jossey-Bass.

ARMOR, D. J. (1974) "Theta reliability and factor scaling," pp. 17-50 in H. L. Costner (ed.) Sociological Methodology 1973-1974. San Francisco: Jossey-Bass.

BALCH, G. I. (1974) "Multiple indicators in survey research: the concept 'sense of political efficacy.'" Political Methodology 1: 1-44.

BENTLER, P. M. (1969) "Alpha-maximized factor analysis (alphamax): its relation to alpha and canonical-factor analysis." Psychometrika 33: 335-346.

——— D. N. JACKSON, and S. J. MESSICK (1972) "A rose by any other name." Psychological Bulletin 77: 109-113.

BLALOCK, H. M. (1968) "The measurement problem," pp. 5-27 in H. M. Blalock and A. Blalock (eds.) Methodology in Social Research. New York: McGraw-Hill.

BOHRNSTEDT, G. W. (forthcoming) "Measurement," in J. Wright and P. Rossi (eds.) Handbook of Survey Research. New York: Academic Press.

——— (1970) "Reliability and validity assessment in attitude measurement," pp. 80-99 in G. F. Summer (ed.) Attitude Measurement. Chicago: Rand McNally.

——— (1969) "A quick method for determining the reliability and validity of multiple-item scales." American Sociological Review 34: 542-548.

BROWN, W. (1910) "Some experimental results in the correlation of mental abilities." British Journal of Psychology 3: 296-322.

CAMPBELL, A., P. E. CONVERSE, W. E. MILLER, and D. E. STOKES (1960) The American Voter. New York: John Wiley.

CAMPBELL, D. T. and D. W. FISKE (1959) "Convergent and discriminant validation by the multitrait-multimethod matrix." Psychological Bulletin 56: 85-105.

CARMINES, E. G. (1978) "Psychological origins of adolescent political attitudes: self-esteem, political salience, and political involvement." American Politics Quarterly 6: 167-186.

——— and R. A. ZELLER (1974) "On establishing the empirical dimensionality of theoretical terms: an analytic example." Political Methodology 1: 75-96.

CRONBACH, L. J. (1971) "Test Validation," pp. 443-507 in R. L. Thorndike (ed.) Educational Measurement. Washington, DC: American Council on Education.

——— (1951) "Coefficient alpha and the internal structure of tests." Psychometrika 16: 297-334.

——— and P. E. MEEHL (1955) "Construct validity in psychological tests." Psychological Bulletin 52: 281-302.

56

CURTIS, R. F. and E. F. JACKSON (1962) "Multiple indicators in survey research." American Journal of Sociology 68: 195-204.

ERIKSON, R. S. (1978) "Analyzing one variable—three wave panel data: a comparison of two models." Political Methodology 5: 151-166.

GREENE, V. and E. G. CARMINES (forthcoming) "Assessing the reliability of linear composites," in K. F. Schuessler (ed.) Sociological Methodology 1980. San Francisco: Jossey-Bass.

HARMAN, H. H. (1976) Modern Factor Analysis. Chicago: University of Chicago Press.

HEISE, D. R. (1974) "Some issues in sociological measurement," pp. 1-16 in H. L. Costner (ed.) Sociological Methodology 1973-1974. San Francisco: Jossey-Bass.

——— (1969) "Separating reliability and stability in test-retest correlations." American Sociological Review 34: 93-101.

——— and G. W. BOHRNSTEDT (1970) "Validity, invalidity, and reliability," pp. 104-129 in E. F. Borgatta and G. W. Bohrnstedt (eds.) Sociological Methodology 1970. San Francisco: Jossey-Bass.

HOFSTETTER, C. R. (1971) "The amateur politician: a problem in construct validation." Midwest Journal of Political Science 15: 31-56.

JONES, L. V. (1971) "The nature of measurement," pp. 335-355 in R. L. Thorndike (ed.) Educational Measurement (2d ed.). Washington, DC: American Council on Education.

JÖRESKOG, K. G. (1971) "Statistical analysis of sets of congeneric tests." Psychometrika 36: 109-133.

KIM, J. and C. W. MUELLER (1978a) Introduction to Factor Analysis: What It Is and How To Do It. Beverly Hills, CA: Sage.

——— (1978b) Factor Analysis: Statistical Methods and Practical Issues. Beverly Hills, CA: Sage.

KUDER, G. F. and M. W. RICHARDSON (1937) "The theory of the estimation of test reliability." Psychometrika 2: 151-160.

LORD, F. M. and M. R. NOVICK (1968) Statistical Theories of Mental Test Scores. Reading, MA: Addison-Wesley.

NOVICK, M. and G. LEWIS (1967) "Coefficient alpha and the reliability of composite measurements." Psychometrika 32: 1-13.

NUNNALLY, J. C. (1978) Psychometric Theory. New York: McGraw-Hill.

——— (1964) Educational Measurement and Evaluation. New York: McGraw-Hill.

RILEY, M. W. (1963) Sociological Research: A Case Approach. New York: Harcourt Brace Jovanovich.

RORER, L. G. (1965) "The great response-style myth." Psychological Bulletin 63: 129-156.

ROSENBERG, M. (1965) Society and the Adolescent Self Image. Princeton, NJ: Princeton University Press.

SEEMAN, M. (1959) "On the meaning of alienation." American Sociological Review 24: 783-791.

SMITH, K. W. (1974a) "On estimating the reliability of composite indexes through factor analysis." Sociological Methods and Research 4: 485-510.

———— (1974b) "Forming composite scales and estimating their validity through factor analysis." Social Forces 53: 168-180.

SPEARMAN, C. (1910) "Correlation calculated from faulty data." British Journal of Psychology 3: 271-295.

STANLEY, J. C. (1971) "Reliability," pp. 356-442 in R. L. Thorndike (ed.) Educational Measurement. Washington, DC: American Council on Education.

STEVENS, S. S. (1951) "Mathematics, measurement and psychophysics," pp. 1-49 in S. S. Stevens (ed.) Handbook of Experimental Psychology. New York: John Wiley.

SULLIVAN, J. L. (1974) "Multiple indicators: some criteria of selection," pp. 243-269 in H. M. Blalock (ed.) Measurement in the Social Sciences: Theories and Strategies. Chicago: AVC.

———— (1971) "Multiple indicators in complex causal models," pp. 327-334 in H. M. Blalock (ed.) Causal Models in the Social Sciences. Chicago: AVC.

———— and S. FELDMAN (1979) Multiple Indicators: An Introduction. Beverly Hills, CA: Sage.

WERTS, C. E. and R. N. LINN (1970) "Cautions in applying various procedures for determining the reliability and validity of multiple-item scales." American Sociological Review 35: 757-759.

WHEATON, B., B. MUTHEN, D. F. ALWIN, and G. F. SUMMERS (1977) "Assessing reliability and stability in panel models," pp. 84-136 in D. R. Heise (ed.) Sociological Methodology 1977. San Francisco: Jossey-Bass.

WILEY, D. E. and J. E. WILEY (1970) "The estimation of measurement error in panel data." American Sociological Review 35: 112-116.

WILEY, J. A. and M. G. WILEY (1974) "A note on correlated errors in repeated measurements." Sociological Methods and Research 3: 172-188.

ZELLER, R. A. and E. G. CARMINES (forthcoming) Measurement in the Social Sciences: The Link Between Theory and Data. New York: Cambridge University Press.

———— (1976) "Factor scaling, external consistency, and the measurement of theoretical constructs." Political Methodology 3: 215-252.

APPENDIX

The Place of Factor Analysis
in Reliability and Validity Assessment

Since factor analysis is often used to construct scales in the social sciences, this appendix will discuss how this statistical technique can be used to assess the reliability of multiple-item measures. We will also briefly discuss and illustrate the uses and limitations of factor analysis in assessing the validity of empirical measurement.[16]

Factor Analysis and Reliability Estimation

In discussing the various methods for assessing reliability, we noted that one of the assumptions underlying these methods is that the items in the scale are parallel, which implies that the items measure a single phenomenon equally. As Armor (1974) observes, this suggests that there are two conditions under which real data can violate these assumptions: if the items measure a single phenomenon unequally or if the items measure more than one concept equally or unequally.

Factor analysis is explicitly designed to cope with both of these situations. Essentially factor analysis consists of a variety of statistical methods for discovering clusters of interrelated variables.[17] It is typically the case that more than one of these clusters, or factors, underlies a set of items. Each factor is defined by those items that are more highly correlated with each other than with the other items. A statistical indication of the extent to which each item is correlated with each factor is given by the factor loading. In other words, the higher the factor loading, the more the particular item contributes to the given factor. Thus, factor analysis also explicitly takes into consideration the fact that the items measure a factor unequally.

In sum, reliability coefficients based on factor analysis are not as restrictive as those methods for estimating reliability that assume parallel items. We shall now discuss two of the more popular of these coefficients.

THETA

Coefficient theta can be easily understood once we consider in greater detail principal components, the factor analysis model on which this reliability coefficient is based. Given a set of items in which there are no perfect intercorrelations, a principal-component analysis will yield as many components as there are items. The components are extracted in decreasing order of importance in terms of the amount of variance associated with each component. That is, the first component accounts for the largest proportion of variance among the items, the second component for the second largest proportion that is independent of the first component, and so on. Corresponding to each of these components is a series of loadings. The size of these loadings gives an indication of the contribution that the item makes to each component. Since the components are extracted in decreasing order of importance, it follows that the sum of (and average of) the squared loadings (i.e., the eigenvalue) will be higher for the first components than for the last extracted components. Thus, there is a negative relationship between the eigenvalue of a component and when that component was extracted. For example, the third extracted component always has an eigenvalue that is less than the second component and greater than the fourth component.

Given these properties of principal components, what should one expect if a set of items is measuring a single phenomenon? Several aspects of the extracted (i.e., unrotated) factor matrix could support this hypothesis: (1) the first extracted component should explain a large proportion of the variance in the items (say > 40%); (2) subsequent components should explain fairly equal proportions of the remaining variance except for a gradual decrease; (3) all or most of the items should have substantial loadings on the first component (say > .3); and (4) all or most of the items should have higher loadings on the first component than on subsequent components.

Now consider the alternative situation in which the researcher has hypothesized that a set of items measures more than a single phenomenon. In this case, a principal-component analysis of the items should meet the following conditions: (1) the number of statistically meaningful components should equal the number of hypothesized phenomena; (2) after rotation, specific items should have higher factor loadings on the hypothesized relevant component than on other components; and (3) components extracted subsequent to the number of hypothesized components should be statistically unimportant and substantively uninterpretable.

When a set of items is measuring more than a single underlying phenomenon, it is often necessary to rotate the extracted components in order for them to be optimally interpretable. At this point, the researcher has two options in constructing scales. First, scales can be computed directly from the rotated factor structure. Alternatively, subsets of items defining each of the rotated components can be refactored according to the principal-component procedure.

However the items and their corresponding weights are chosen, the reliability of the resulting scale can be estimated using the following formula for theta:

$$\theta = (N/N - 1)(1 - 1/\lambda_1) \qquad [23]$$

where θ represents theta; N equals the number of items; and λ_1 is the largest (i.e., the first) eigenvalue. Theta lends itself to many different interpretations but it is understood most simply as being a special case of Cronbach's alpha. Specifically, theta is the alpha coefficient for a scale in which the weighting vector has been chosen so as to make alpha a maximum. In other words, theta may be considered a maximized alpha coefficient (Greene and Carmines, forthcoming).

OMEGA

Another estimate of reliability for linear scales that has gained some popularity is omega, a reliability coefficient introduced by Heise and Bohrnstedt (1970). Omega is based on the common factor analysis model. In this model, unities have been replaced by communality estimates in the main diagonal of the correlation matrix prior to factoring. Omega takes the general form:

$$\Omega = 1 - (\Sigma\sigma_i^2 - \Sigma\sigma_i^2 h_i^2)/(\Sigma\Sigma\sigma_{x_i x_j}) \qquad [24]$$

where Ω is omega; σ_i^2 is equal to the variance of the ith item; h_i^2 is equal to the communality of the ith item; and $\Sigma\Sigma\sigma_{x_i x_j}$ is the sum of the covariances among the items. If one is working with correlations, then the formula for omega reduces to:

$$\Omega = 1 - (a - \Sigma h_i^2)/(a + 2b) \qquad [25]$$

where a is equal to the number of items and b is the sum of the correlations among the items.

There are three important diffences between omega and theta (Armor, 1974). First, they are based on different factor-analytic models. Theta is grounded in the principal-components model whereas omega is based on the common factor analysis model. This means that one always uses 1.0's in the main diagonal to compute the eigenvalues on which theta is based but the value of omega depends, in part, on communalities, which are estimated quantities not fixed ones. This is another way of saying that because omega is based on estimated communalities, there is an element of indeterminancy in its calculation that is not present in theta. Finally, unlike theta, "omega does not assess the reliability of separate scales in the event of multiple dimensions" (Armor, 1974: 47). Rather, omega provides a coefficient that estimates the reliability of all the common factors in a given item set.

We should note, finally, the relationship among theta, omega, and alpha. If the items making up the scale are parallel measurements, then all three coefficients will be equal to one another and will equal the reliability of the scale. Otherwise, the following order will hold: alpha $<$ theta $<$ omega. Thus, we again see that alpha is a *lower bound* for the reliability of multiitem scales. And of these three internal consistency coefficients, omega provides the highest estimate of reliability—that is, the *closest estimate* to the true reliability of the measure. (For further discussion of these reliability coefficients, see Greene and Carmines, forthcoming.)

Factor Analysis and Construct Validity

Factor analysis can also be useful for assessing the validity of empirical measures (Nunally, 1978). However, if the results of a factor analysis are interpreted without theoretical guidance, it can lead to misleading conclusions concerning the validity of measuring instruments. In order to illustrate the uses and especially the limitations of assessing construct validity through factor analysis, we will focus on Rosenberg's (1965) conceptualization and measurement of self-esteem. Rosenberg defines self-esteem as the overall attitude that a person maintains with regard to his own worth and importance. Rosenberg conceptualizes self-esteem as a unitary personal predisposition, and he constructed 10 items designed to measure this trait. The data for this analysis come from a study of the relationship between personality traits and political attitudes among high school students (Carmines, 1978).

FACTOR-ANALYTIC INTERPRETATIONS OF SELF-ESTEEM

A correlation matrix of the 10 items used to measure self-esteem is presented in Table 3. On the whole, the items intercorrelate positively, consistently, and significantly. But do the items form a single dimension of self-esteem?

A common factor (principal axes) analysis (using SMC's in the main diagonal) of the items is shown in Table 4. Within a strict factor-analytic framework, Rosenberg's conceptualization implies that we should observe a unifactorial structure. However, the results of the factor analysis do not clearly support this presumption. Rather, the factor solution indicates that there are two substantial empirical factors that underlie these data. Further, when these two factors are rotated to a varimax solution, as shown in Table 4, they show a fairly distinct clustering of items. Factor I is defined principally by items 1, 3, 5, 8, and 10 while items 2, 4, 6, 7, and 9 most clearly define factor II. We may refer to factor I as the *positive self-esteem* factor, since those items that load most strongly on it are reflective of a positive, favorable attitude toward the self. For example, one of these items states, "I feel that I'm a person of worth, at least on an equal place with others." By contrast, those items that most clearly define factor II have in common a negative, unfavorable reference to the self. For example, the item that loads highest on factor II states, "At times I think I am no good at all." We may refer to factor II, therefore, as the *negative self-esteem* factor. These

TABLE 3
Correlation Matrix of Self-Esteem Items[a]

Items	1	2	3	4	5	6	7	8	9	10
1	—	.185	.451	.399	.413	.263	.394	.352	.361	.204
2		—	.048*	.209	.248	.246	.230	.050*	.277	.270
3			—	.350	.399	.209	.381	.427	.276	.332
4				—	.369	.415	.469	.280	.358	.221
5					—	.338	.446	.457	.317	.425
6						—	.474	.214	.502	.189
7							—	.315	.577	.311
8								—	.299	.374
9									—	.233
10										—

a. N = 340.
*p $>$ .05. For all other correlations in Table p $<$ .001.
1. I feel that I have a number of good qualities.[b]
2. I wish I could have more respect for myself.[c]
3. I feel that I'm a person of worth, at least on an equal plane with others.
4. I feel I do not have much to be proud of.
5. I take a positive attitude toward myself.
6. I certainly feel useless at times.
7. All in all, I'm inclined to feel that I am a failure.
8. I am able to do things as well as most other people.
9. At times I think I am no good at all.
10. On the whole, I am satisfied with myself.
b. Response categories for items are: (1) Never true, (2) Seldom true, (3) Sometimes true, (4) Often true, (5) Almost always true.
c. Items 2, 4, 6, 7, and 9 have been reflected such that higher scores indicate higher self-esteem.

empirical factors of self-esteem are not polar opposites. Rather, the results of the factor analysis indicate that the dimensions are definitely distinguishable from one another, forming as they do separate identifiable factors.

Moreover, when we factor analyze the two sets of items separately, one and only one substantial factor emerges for each dimension of self-esteem (see Table 5). Further, the items forming these factors show fairly strong loadings on their respective factors. That is, the negative self-esteem items have loadings ranging from .351 to .757 on their principal factor, as shown in Table 5. This analysis offers strong support for the bidimensionality of self-esteem.

TABLE 4
Factor Loadings of the Self-Esteem Items

Items[a]	Extracted			Rotated		
	I	II	h	I	II	h
1	.590	.109	.360	.495[b]	.339	.360
2	.328	−.176	.138	.109	.356	.138
3	.581	.314	.436	.633	.187	.436
4	.600	−.085	.367	.365	.483	.367
5	.669	.198	.487	.614	.332	.487
6	.577	−.346	.453	.165	.653	.453
7	.731	−.202	.575	.376	.659	.575
8	.549	.387	.451	.662	.113	.451
9	.640	−.359	.539	.200	.706	.539
10	.480	.196	.269	.478	.200	.269
Eigenvalue	3.410	.666		2.043	2.032	
Percent of Variance	.341	.067	.408	.204	.203	.407

a. For an exposition of items, see Table 3.
b. The underlined factor loading indicates which of the factors each item loads higher on.

AN ALTERNATIVE INTERPRETATION
OF THE TWO-FACTOR SOLUTION

The factor analyses of Rosenberg's self-esteem scale have indicated that the items do not necessarily form a single empirical dimension of self-esteem but rather that they may reflect two distinct components of the self-image. Because of the items that tended to define each factor, we labeled one of these components the positive self-esteem factor while we referred to the other component as the negative self-esteem factor. We now want to consider an alternative interpretation of the two-factor solution. Specifically, we want to consider the possibility that the dual dimensionality of self-esteem is a function of nonrandom measurement error: namely, response set among the two sets of scale items.

Response set may be defined as the general tendency to respond to interview or questionnaire items in a particular manner, irre-

TABLE 5
Factor Loadings of Positive and Negative Self-Esteem
Items Factored Separately

Positive Self-Esteem Items

Item	Factor Loading	h^2
1	.568	.323
3	.651	.424
5	.699	.489
8	.658	.433
10	.524	.275

Negative Self-Esteem Items

Item	Factor Loading	h^2
2	.351	.123
4	.577	.333
6	.674	.454
7	.757	.573
9	.727	.528

spective of their content. Clearly, this is a very real possibility in the present case, for the items forming each of the dimensions of self-esteem are worded in a similar manner. That is, the items which load higher on the positive self-esteem factor are all worded in a positive direction while those loading higher on the negative self-esteem factor are all worded in a negative direction. Given this situation, it is not unusual to find somewhat higher correlations among items which are worded in the same direction than among items which differ in the direction of their wording. This, of course, is precisely what we observed in the intercorrelations among the self-esteem items. Notice also that the positive and negative signs of the factor loadings on the second principal factor in the un-rotated structure are representative of the positive and negative wording of the items.

In addition, since factor analysis does nothing more than re-define and simplify the correlation matrix, we would also expect that response set among items would contaminate the factor structure of those items. A two-factor empirical solution, in other words, does not invariably indicate that the two factors measure two separate theoretical concepts. It may also be an indication that the items are an empirical representation of a single concept, self-esteem, with the second factor due to a method artifact such as response set. Let us assume, for the moment, that the proper interpretation is a single theoretical concept with response set producing the second factor. In this case, the first factor obtained from the principal-factor solution represents theoretically valid variance while the second factor represents systematic error variance. The point is that a factor analysis itself cannot differentiate between these two interpretations, since it only reflects the differential pattern of correlations among the scale items.

In summary, the factor analysis of the scale items does not provide unambiguous, and even less unimpeachable, evidence of the theoretical dimensionality underlying these self-esteem items. On the contrary, since the bifactorial structure can be a function of a single theoretical dimension which is contaminated by a method artifact as well as being indicative of two separate, substantive dimensions, the factor analysis leaves the theoretical structure of self-esteem indeterminate.

RESOLVING THE ALTERNATIVE INTERPRETATION OF THE TWO-FACTOR SOLUTION

Factor analysis does not resolve the issue of the conceptual/theoretical structure of Rosenberg's self-esteem scale. Following the logic of construct validation, the appropriate procedure is to compare the correlations of each empirical dimension of self-esteem with a set of theoretically relevant external variables. If the positive and negative self-esteem factors measure different components of the self-image, they should relate differentially to at least some of these external variables. If, on the other hand, the factors measure a single dimension of self-esteem with the bifactorial structure being due to a method artifact, the two factors should relate similarly to these theoretically relevant variables. By following this procedure, we will be able to evaluate the theoretical structure of self-esteem.

TABLE 6
Correlations between Positive and Negative Self-Esteem Scales and External Variables

External Variable	N	Positive Self-Esteem Factor[a]	Negative Self-Esteem Factor[b]	Difference Between Correlations
Socioeconomic Background Factors				
Father's Education	198	.17**	.15**	.02
Mother's Education	208	.11***	.08	.03
Father's Occupation	198	.12***	.08	.04
Psychological Predispositions				
Personal Control	334	.31*	.33*	−.02
Anomie	340	−.54*	−.49	.05
Trust-in-People	340	.24*	.25*	−.01
Self-Anchoring Scale:				
Present	219	.16**	.14***	.02
Future	216	.18**	.14***	.04
Intelligence	272	.22*	.24*	−.02
Social and Political Attitudes				
Participation in School Activities	338	.14**	.11***	.03
Participation in Community Activities	228	.05	.02	.03
Political Efficacy	334	.18*	.22*	−.04
Political Cynicism	331	−.09***	−.13**	.04
Knowledge of Political Authorities	331	.14**	.09***	.05
Knowledge of Government Services	333	.12***	.10***	.02
Understanding of Democratic Principles	334	.16**	.13**	.03

a. The positive self-esteem items were unit weighted to form a composite scale.
b. The negative self-esteem items were unit weighted to form a composite scale. These items were reflected such that higher scores indicate higher self-esteem.

*p $<$ .001.
**p $<$ .01.
***p $<$ .05.

Table 6 presents the correlations between each dimension of self-esteem and 16 external variables. These variables cover three broad substantive areas: socioeconomic background factors, other psychological predispositions, and social and political attitudes. Almost all of the correlations are statistically significant (at the .05 level) and a majority of them seem to be substantively important as well. The positive and negative self-esteem scales, in other words, seem to capture a salient dimension of the adolescent's self-image. But these factors seem to tap the same, rather than different, dimensions, for their correlation with these theoretically relevant external variables are almost identical to one another in terms of direction, strength, and consistency. Indeed, the average difference between correlations across all 16 variables is approximately .03, with the highest difference being .05. None of these differences is statistically significant (at even the .25 level), and it would be extremely difficult to attach theoretical importance to the differences as well.

In summary, while the factor analysis left the theoretical structure of the self-esteem items indeterminate, the evidence provided by an analysis of their construct validity leads to a more definitive conclusion: namely, that the items measure a single theoretical dimension of self-esteem. The two-factor solution, therefore, offers only spurious evidence for the dual theoretical dimensionality of self-esteem. The more appropriate interpretation is that the bifactorial structure of the items is a function of a single theoretical dimension of self-esteem that is contaminated by a method artifact, response set.

Conclusion

This appendix has discussed the relation of factor analysis to reliability and validity assessment. As we have seen, there is a very close connection between factor analysis and reliability assessment. In particular, reliability coefficients derived from factor analysis models make less stringent assumptions about items than alpha-based reliability which presumes that the items are parallel measures.

The use of factor analysis in assessing validity is much more of a two-edged sword. While it can be useful for this purpose, factor analysis does not always lead to unambiguous inferences concerning the underlying *theoretical* dimensionality of a set of items. Instead, naive and simplistic interpretation of factor structures can be misleading in terms of determining the substantive nature of empirical measures. We have seen how response set can artificially produce an inference of two underlying dimensions when in fact there is only one. *Any method artifact that can systematically alter the correlations among items may produce this kind of faulty inference.*

In summary, while factor analysis is quite useful for assessing the reliability and validity of empirical measures, it is properly seen as a tool of theoretical analysis, not as a replacement for it. Used in this more modest role, factor analysis can aid in the development and assessment of empirical measurements.

EDWARD G. CARMINES *is Rudy Professor of Political Science at Indiana University, Bloomington. He received his Ph.D. from the State University of New York at Buffalo. His primary research interests are in American politics and methodology, and he has published articles in these areas in various journals, including the* American Political Science Review, Journal of Politics, *and* American Journal of Political Science. *He is the coauthor, with Richard A. Zeller, of* Statistical Analysis of Social Data *and* Measurement in the Social Sciences: The Link Between Theory and Data, *and, with James A. Stimson, of* Issue Evolution. *His current research focuses on the origins, evolution, and resolution of political issues in American politics.*

RICHARD A. ZELLER *is currently Professor of Sociology at Bowling Green State University, Bowling Green. He received his Ph.D. in 1972 from the University of Wisconsin, Madison. His major professional interests are research methodology, statistics, and measurement reliability and validity. He has coauthored three books and published articles in* Sociological Methods and Research, Journal of Social Psychology, International Encyclopedia of Education, Professional Psychology, *and* Teaching Sociology. *Dr. Zeller serves as consultant to NSF, MINH, IDRC, and the Case Western Reserve University; and is International Consultant for the Augustine/Zeller Group where he has advised Fortune 500 companies on marketing policy.*

CPSIA information can be obtained
at www.ICGtesting.com
Printed in the USA
FSHW022322071221
86584FS